King's Daughters Series:
I THINK I LIKE MY NATURAL HAIR

STEPHANIE SHIDER

King's Daughters Series:

I Think I Like My Natural Hair

Copyright © 2015 Stephanie Shider

ISBN- 9781713299400

Printed in the United States

DEDICATION

This book is dedicated to all the men and women who struggle to find their identity and love the way God has made them! Enjoy! I hope you find strength in loving yourself entirely as the original human being God designed you to be. Dare to be you! Securely and Confidently in Christ. In Jesus' Name I pray Amen.

ACKNOWLEDGEMENTS

Special thanks to Nadia DeLane for her support and creative input to the design of this book. Your words and passion for this topic inspired me.

Thank you to my best friend since the 4th grade, Sherrell, who kept pushing and prodding me about the completion of this book. Thank you! Thank You! Thank You! For the encouragement, support and reading all of the rough copies to give me your sister girl insight on the content. Much appreciated. You just don't know!

Thank you to my aunt Jackie! One of my favorite aunts who loved and supported me through my first editing stage! You made the book what it is! Your way with words and encouragement as my family catapulted me to the next stage. I don't know what I would have done without you during this process.

Thank you to my daughter Mya who inspires and pushes me every day to be a better mother and female role model who is confident in who she is in Christ, so she too can be confident in the godly, young lady father God desires her to be and is.

Special thanks to my handsome, sexy chocolate husband who constantly reminded me to continue and not give up on this project. Thank you for your constant love and support. Your words of encouragement and understanding of who I am and not being afraid to back me up fills me. This entire journey I have been on is priceless! Your love amazes me and I appreciate you. You as my king and me as your queen. "Love never fails". I love you Ty!

Thank you to my parents Barbara and James Bridgers and Keith and Tracy Shider. Thank you James and Barbara for being there for me NO MATTER WHAT! Your love and continuous support, even when you may not have understood me is priceless! Having a home you know you can always come to and be poured into and filled with love is peace and joy like none other. Thank you Mom Shider for encouraging me to get it done or else it never will and Pop Shider for being a constant present support and encourager.

Last but not least, to my Abba, Father, for giving me the time and energy to write this book to be a blessing to any and everyone who reads it. I'm in Awe of EVERYTHING that you Do! Your love is AMAZING and encompassing! I am forever grateful to how you've been a blessing to me and how you allow me to continue to be a blessing towards others. I pray that everyone who reads this love letter I wrote to you and sees how you've been able to deliver me from my lack of love for myself, will go on their own inward journey of finding your love as oh so encompassing so they can begin their inward love journey towards you as well! Love you much! You're AMAZING!

Love your daughter, Stephanie

CONTENTS

FOREWARD

Dear Abba,

I love the way you've expressed your love for us aesthetically. When I go to a park to acknowledge your creativity I am humbled. Look at the body of water and how the light from your sun glistens on its many waves. Hear the rhythm of the wind; its highs and lows blowing a song from the mouth of your trees. Most of its rhythm will travel places I have not gone. See how superior the ducks are, as if you are whispering to them about my insecurities. As I stand back in awe of your creation: the trees, the breeze, the body of water, the ducks, the grass, and the hills, the sun in the sky, the clouds, and the dust are PERFECT. Are you satisfied with your PERFECT work? Or do you smile at its imperfection? Which? IF you made everything PERFECT, why'd you forget about me?

The above excerpt is from a letter I wrote to God. I had set out to conceive a book, 'Dear Abba', that would be an epistolary novel navigating the prayers of a broken black man to God. Though it is almost redundant to use broken as an adjective for black people in America as the two are practically simultaneous. But that might be an entirely different issue than the one explored in this book. Stephanie's work seeks to expose the complex ideology imposed upon people of color that says: Africans are, by nature, cosmetically inferior to their European counterparts. This 'idea' has especially had an effect on our sisters who must contest centuries of assimilationist like practices by their predecessors to emulate Eurocentric woman in order to appear less threatening and even more attractive in America.

This book is meeting the contemporary woman of color plagued by inherited practices of self-hatred such as: skin lightening, hair weaving and relaxing, where she is to tell her what she is doing, how she got there, and to introduce her to ways she can begin taking off the mask in an effort to begin embracing her natural beauty. Stephanie has been brave in tackling an issue many believe is archaic in our 'progressive-liberalist' world where 'blonde' haired Beyoncé is beautiful; but I believe this book will spark the conversation that will begin to heal and empower our women from within. We started somewhere, and we were ALREADY beautiful there.

Enjoy,

Tylie Shider

Intro: I HIDE by Tee Emmanuel

As I hide behind the words I lied on.
I smile and hide the pain that I feared on.
Don't think I'm crazy when I say, I feel like a joker.
But people take me as a joke.
I'm not saying people can't never take me seriously.
But only I can't take myself serious. Due to
the fact that only I know how I'm feeling.
What I WANT to say. As I hide behind the
words I lied on. Feeling as if I've been cursed
the way I am. Always hiding.
Feeling like people are always out to get me.
I'm scared.
Scared of myself.
Scared that one day that I will die.
But not....natural causes.
Scared of the thoughts of me.
The thoughts that escape my mind that
express itself through the clench of my jaw.
That hole in my mind.
The violence I want to do.
The self-mutilation I've done to this
chocolate skin.
But I hide.
Like a joker people take me as a joke.
Sometimes I hide behind the words I lie on.
But no one knows until you see the self-
damage I've done to myself.
The physical, mental and emotional.

But I'm perfectly fine I just continue to...

INTRODUCTION

"You're pretty for a brown-skinned girl." Excuse me! Did I hear you correctly? What exactly do you mean by that? Pretty for a brown-skinned girl? Why can't I just be pretty? Really? Do you have to have light skin and long hair in order to truly be considered beautiful? Are we still fighting our self-worth and identity because of the institutionalized racism that unfortunately still goes on today? Do I really have to fight this temptation of putting long horse hair in my head because of my inability to find my true beauty within myself? My true self. Why do I have to feel this way? Where does this come from?

Why can't black men love themselves enough to love the women that they come from? Why can't men, period, find the true beauty of a black woman attractive without the expenditures that come from latex, pulling up, putting on and sucking in the areas that are deemed to be unworthy of being left alone since the J-Lo's, Beyonce's and Halle Berry's of the world have fortunately made it acceptable to embrace certain curves on your body and to be beautiful with the minimal hair that you may be blessed to have. Why, why, why do I have to feel this way or think about these things that in reality are so insignificant to all the other challenges I must go through throughout my daily life experience? Is something really going to give? Do I really have to fight with myself about what style of dress I want to represent today? Who deemed this to be so important and why are many of us stuck there, thinking the way we look on the outside is so much more important than the attitude we carry within? Certainly, a so called "pretty" face with a jacked-up attitude is not more acceptable than someone who is considered "okay" to the dominant culture with a beautiful and loving spirit to all whom she encounters. Unfortunately, in today's society, this is the case. More often, what you look like on the outside is more favorable than the spirit or attitude you carry within. When did your self-worth depend on how much money you have, what you wear, what you drive and even more importantly to our society, the color of your skin and how close it resembles the European culture that is considered to be dominant in our society today? I'm not quite sure when it originated. However, I'm sure the technology and connection to the world through the various media forms have contributed to this ideal.

I'm sure in one way or another, many, if not all of these questions have circled through your mind in your adolescent to adult years of living. Whether it was the shocking and very unexpected comment that "you were pretty for a brown skin girl" by the opposite sex who was no lighter than you himself or the constant bombardment of magazines, commercials, videos and T.V. shows that indirectly show you what is considered beautiful compared to what is not. Our self-worth was attacked by our everyday experiences living in a world that put (and continues to put) so much emphasis on the outside appearance vs. what is actually truly important.

What could possibly be more important than the wealth that I accumulate that contributes to how many shoes I have in my closet, the brand of clothes I wear, where I live, and how many electronic gadgets I have compared to the next person, and most importantly the car that I drive? I don't know. Maybe the answer comes from the verse where Peter states in 1 Peter 3:3:

Whose adorning let it not be that outward adorning of plaiting the hair, and of wearing of gold, or of putting on of apparel; But let it be the hidden man of the heart, in that which is not corruptible, even the ornament of a meek and quiet spirit, which is in the sight of God of great price.

I don't know about you, but the translation to me seems to blatantly state that although God has taken a great deal of time to create us individually and magnificently, His greatest concern is not about how much money we have or what we may look like on the outside, however, what is most important is our heart and the quiet and humble spirit that comes from within: our character. So, why do we put so much emphasis on something that God doesn't put emphasis on? Surely if God is not that concerned about it, then that emphasis on the materialistic and outward appearance comes from another source. Sure, God wants us to have His best as we do represent Him. However, it isn't the end all and be all of our life's existence.

Yet I know, at times, this verse can be taken so far by various types of people. Some groups of people in religious circles have even made it a style of life whereas you would be frowned upon, as a woman, if you wore pants, makeup, and did any form of elaborate style to your hair. I can attest to the fact that it truly does bring your life into a different focus; A focus that doesn't emphasize the materialistic or worldly ideas of what beauty is, but truly reflects on the inner man (or woman) and inner character that he/she possesses. The new focus would undoubtedly be so much more attractive than something as depleting and transforming as one's outward appearance.

However, does that mean you shouldn't focus on your outward appearance altogether? Surely not taking care of yourself is totally different than putting too much emphasis on your outward appearance. From experience, I know about the desire to go against conforming to our society. This can truly affect your sense of self and can easily be taken out of context if you lean too far left or too far right. I remember when I arrived at a point in my life where I didn't want to be defined by my outward appearance any longer. I wanted people to focus on who I was on the inside, and not who they thought I was at first glance. I wanted my inward character and beauty to outshine anything people saw. It became my mission to work on my inner woman more and not what I looked like to people.

CHAPTER 1
THE ROOT

It was fourth grade when my best friend Shelby arrived to school from Trinidad. She was the sweet and quiet "new girl". I knew if I were to be the new student within a brand-new country, I would like for someone to reach out to me. So, it became my plight in life, as a 4th grade student, to embrace her as I would want someone to embrace me.

Little did I know this would be a challenge that I would begin to embark on as I began, for the first time in my young adolescent years, to question my worth, identity and belonging as a young African American girl. Who knew I was going to be challenged with the length of my hair, color of my skin and a longing to be accepted for who I was at this age? Who was prepared to entertain and console the feelings I would feel when my so called Caucasian friends seemed to toss me aside for the next cute little black girl who was obviously deemed to be more pretty and "friend" worthy than I was due to her longer hair and lighter skin. Is this really taking place? Maybe I'm over exaggerating and that's not what was happening at all. Maybe I'm just being too sensitive about the whole matter and those emotions are not completely true. But hold on, they just dismissed me again after playing with Shelby's hair during break, "because black hair is so different and exciting to play with, but oh, Stephanie, yours is not long enough to put in the pretty pigtails that we are able to put Shelby's in. Even if we tried, it doesn't look the same and

Shelby's hair looks so much cuter."

NOW, as a thirty-year-old mother and wife, I'm not sure if that's exactly how that specific event played out. However, for me to remember the exact grade and to have a picture in my mind of that specific scene, not to mention remembering how I felt, this event had obviously made a significant impact on my life. It also marked the unexpected and new found journey I had in dealing with and managing my hair which I undoubtedly trigger to this specific event that had me feeling unaccepted because of the length and style of my hair. If I knew, at that age, that I shouldn't have looked to be accepted for the way I styled my hair or how long it was, I might have been able to press myself through and begin to love myself for me, regardless of how anyone else felt or treated me because of it. However juvenile and extremely shallow this event and events like this were that took place in my life, they inevitably had long lasting impressions that effected my self-worth even as a young girl.

My mother was the first one to notice and be shocked by my unexpected behavior. Although she says I was five when we started having the Battles of the Hair, I know specifically if the battle started, it inevitably had to start after this mean and hurtful experience. I no longer wanted to settle for the little girl braided and twisted styles that my mother took her time to carefully and neatly create. I wanted to be recognized as having long luxurious hair like Shelby's and also for the mean, rude little girls to be sorry for ever making their nasty comments about my hair that made me feel low and unworthy. Obviously, that didn't happen, and due to my disobedience to my mother by not allowing her to do my hair herself, the expected yet unexpected to me happened and my hair started to break off slowly but surely. My attempts to elongate my hair by putting twists and little balls at the end so that my hair would move when I turned my head failed to actually make it longer and did just the opposite by producing damaged and unmanageable hair (and according to some pictures of the past, looked a hot mess).

Fortunately, yet unfortunately, this little boy named Antonio had a huge crush on me and would find it his mission to get my attention in every way possible. In some sort of way, it affirmed my beauty that someone was taking notice of my self-worth even when I felt so low. I felt appreciated for how I looked and behaved as a young black girl when I was starting to feel unaccepted by some of my Caucasian peers. It never occurred to me, our differences, since the town I grew up in had a little bit of everyone and although we didn't quite look alike, those differences weren't highlighted as far as I could see until this year. However, this little black boy noticed me and validated that he saw something in me that he liked. Although, I pretended to hate it, and detested him as a person, since he was constantly acting a mess and interrupting our important 4th grade lessons, I will forever be grateful that he acknowledged me in his eyes as the little beauty that I was and now wanted to be.

It wasn't always like that, however. Before these days I liked to hang out with the boys and play basketball, jump fences and ride bikes. Being the youngest girl of twin boys and the only girl my age within my suburban neighborhood amongst a bunch of boys made it more likely than not that playing basketball or some other boy-deemed sport would be what I would be playing with my neighbors. It was fun and unobtrusive to not care about little girly things and to put my hair back in a ponytail and forget or willingly downplay how I looked on the outside as most important. At that time, the boys, at least within my neighborhood, didn't measure ones worth or acceptance by how one looked, but by how well you played basketball or by how nice an overall person to hang out and play with you were. Outside appearance, in my opinion, didn't play a major part in the equation for the majority of my adolescent life. My circle included church, family and friends, school and neighborhood. I was always considered a "cute" little girl which I absolutely detested at that age and had no interest in being labeled. Therefore, being cute or finding acceptance in that area was never an issue until it was challenged by my counterparts. I wonder if that's how the darker skin blacks of the past felt when they were challenged with being accepted by their Caucasian counterparts and trying to measure up to what they considered was beautiful?

According to Ayana D. Byrd and Lori L. Tharps book (2011) Hair Story; Untangling the Roots of Black Hair in America, blacks have always been challenged with accepting their African roots, especially when it comes to hair. This was due to the explicit and demanding events that took place within their lives as they were exported and forced to live, work and be ill-treated by their Caucasian counterparts. Loving self as a black American was an idea that was extremely difficult as ideas worked diligently within their social, economic and physical livelihood to cut away any sense of self. The new self that they were forced to embrace in order to be acknowledged as worthy of any type of respect was to look Anglo Saxon by any means possible. The straighter your hair, and lighter your skin, the more privileged and the higher the status you would receive. "Bad hair was the antithesis, namely African hair in its purest form" (Byrd and Tharps, 2011).

I can only imagine the self-hatred, jealousy and envy that went on among black men and women as they immediately became aware of the deliberate act these slave masters took to sell a house slave for five times more than he would a field slave. Their worth quickly became an attainable number as they were sold for 1600 dollars and their lighter counterparts for 5,000. Can you imagine the psychological damage that does to a person? It's no wonder why, "Black people themselves internalized the concept and within their own ranks propagated the notion that darker-skinned Blacks with kinkier hair were less attractive, less intelligent, and worth less than their lighter-hued brothers and sisters." (Byrd and Tharps, 2011).

I guess my assumptions and feelings within my own

discriminatory 4th grade experience can't be that off. My feelings may have very well been legitimate. Although it may have been completely unintentional for my 4th grade peers to desire the lighter skin black girl with the "good-hair", the concept still remains. There is still, unfortunately an underlying meaning of what is considered "pretty" vs. what is not. We all, in some way, use the standards established by Anglo-Saxons to measure ourselves and there are those who use them to judge others. It is so deeply embedded into our country's psyche that we desperately try to convince ourselves otherwise. However, who could blame us when these ideas began to become our norm even amongst blacks themselves. It was a means of survival for some, especially those who were deemed worthy of being better due to their lighter skin.

It is known that free blacks with lighter skin and straighter hair "still enjoyed a sense of freedom and riches unknown by Blacks with darker skin". Historian Joel Williamson writes that these "affluent" and "cultivated" Blacks "enjoyed a status markedly elevated above numbers of the free black mass." To stay in the top elite, they made sure they "segregated themselves in tight-knit communities. From New York to Louisiana, these Black elite protected its position in society by marrying only other Blacks with similar light coloring and straight hair, living in certain neighbor-hoods, and associating professionally and socially with similarly hued people. By the time slavery was officially abolished in 1865, "good" hair and light skin had become the official keys to membership in the Negro elite

(Byrd and Tharps, 2011).

It's inevitable that this concept would eventually start infiltrating the psyche of those who were chosen as the "more elite." It's inevitable that they would no longer want to be associated with those who were considered inferior to their kind and want to disassociate themselves in any way. That would enable them to find some sort of acceptance from the dominant Anglo-Saxon culture in spite of how it made the darker-hued part of the race feel. Therefore, it's inevitable that those who were considered "less than", would start to internalize those concepts as well and begin to "despise and hate ourselves, and all that favors us", lamented one William J. Wilson in an article written in 1853 in Fredrick Douglass' Paper. "Well may we scoff at black skins and woolly heads, since every model set before us for admiration, has a pallid face and flaxen head" (Byrd and Tharps, 2011).

Scoff at and despise we do. Shun away from, demoralize as being "other" or unacceptable or trying to be different is how we often look at anything for that matter that is not Anglo Saxon. Although I commend the Black Power Movement of the 60's and Natural Hair movement of today, the fact still remains that many blacks, still in some shape or form, hate their origin and the responses that they still have to face, even today, for embracing how they were originally created. Rightfully so, as a friend of mine stated after putting chemicals in her hair or wearing numerous styles with weave for several years, "I should not have to explain to my co-workers that I am going to start going natural and the process of my hair and what it would look like." That explanation was followed with an unfavorable comment from a fellow black-male coworker stating, "Oh, so that means your hair is going to be nappy." Even conscious attempts to take back the negative connotation of being called "nappy-headed" and the like through bell Hooks' first children's book "Happy to be Nappy" and another poets book "Nappy Hair", the tone of his comment was meant to be offensive and degrading. In addition, it did not come from another race, which perpetuates the very fact that it is additionally hard to be accepted by our own.

Although much progress has been made in embracing all types of cultures within our world and especially the world of America, beauty and what is looked upon as acceptable or what is normal is still based on some sense of the "Anglo-Saxon" form of beauty whether we like it or not. "The child is taught directly or indirectly that he or she is pretty, just in proportion as the features approximate the Anglo-Saxon standard. Hence the noses must be pinched up. Kinky hair must be subjected to a straightening process- oiled, and puffed, twisted up, tied down, sleeked over and pressed under, or cut off so short that it can't curl, sometimes the natural hair is shaved off and its place supplied by straight wig." (Byrd and Tharps).

These statements came from Martin H. Freeman who voiced his doubts in the Anglo-African magazine after a small population of small blacks began to debate over the effects of light-skin, "good-hair" and the politics of straightening hair being the only option for mainstream society's acceptance (Byrd and Tharps, 2011). Still in this year of 2015, some females have a hard time identifying themselves as just black or African American. Even within the natural hair craze of today, your beauty is measured by the grade of your natural hair! The more mixed you are with another culture the more acceptable. What gives?

We can't displace that much progress has been made in mainstream society about the idea of beauty. The images we see have been more open to displaying women and men of many more nationalities, hairstyles, and sizes. Yet, even at this day and age it seems that you still have to back up, defend, explain or the like, your choice on how you decide to wear your hair as a black American or something even more uncontrollable; the shade of your skin. What is even sadder is that you have to often times defend it within your own race as many darker hued girls stated in the documentary Dark Girls.

Being called ugly, darkie, tar face, and the like is not exactly the affirmation you would like to hear from your own race. One woman states she heard all her peers calling her "dark, black and ugly" so much she just had to give up and just say to herself, "Well I guess I'm just dark, black and ugly", as if there was little to no help of seeing herself otherwise. Another woman even commented that the only reason she would receive attention from a guy is because of her shapely body. How do you help your daughter, niece, or cousin find her beauty within when this ideology is so harsh and wildly received in our society? Especially when it is highlighted amongst the very ones you expect to embrace you like some of our black men who continue to degrade, categorize and emphasize their distaste in particular types of women. Such terms like "butter face" has some women succumbing to detrimental behavior when they are constantly bombarded with the notion that they are only worthy to be with sexually because everything on them looks great "but-her-face." This unfortunate and degrading term leaves them with the idea that they are an object that is to be used for that purpose and that purpose alone. She is regarded as one which can eventually be disposed of until she again is used to serve that very same purpose. An unfortunate story about a woman who dated a Hispanic was told by her boyfriend that she couldn't walk next to him while they were in public. Unbeknownst to her, it was due to the darker shade of her skin. She believed that he loved her, until her mom respectfully declared that "No one who loves you would make you walk behind them in public. He's ashamed of you."

Another particular woman in the documentary felt so dismissed and unable to be loved by anyone that she constantly thought "who would want to love someone like me?" Although someone was able to find her and love her for her. It's still unfortunate that someone has to experience those feelings just because of the negative connotations that are associated with the color of her skin.

Gabriele Douglas couldn't even get a break. She was nationally bashed by some of her own people about the way she kept her hair. What is wrong with this picture? When are we as blacks, African Americans, African descendants, black Americans or whatever we like to be called going to be proud of our heritage? We can't even come together collectively to identify who we really are and how we want to be identified as a whole. "Nigga" is okay for some and rightfully so not for others. Black is unacceptable since we're not all that color. African American is insufficient since we're not Africans who recently migrated to America. Who are we? Our inability to prioritize what is most important for the black race is a direct reflection on why so many couldn't deal with the way Gabriele styled her hair. I understand many were concerned about Gabby's hair because they considered her to be a representation of black women everywhere. Nevertheless, shouldn't we have focused on her ability to be the first African American to win two Olympic gold medals instead? Why was it so hard for us to celebrate this young black lady yet so easy for some of us to try and pull her down at such a crucial age where she is still learning about her own identity? If we are embarrassed about the way others view us when someone represents us with their hair "un-kept" how much more embarrassed are we when others see us criticizing our own when they should in fact be celebrated? We need to get it within our own community before we can help others outside of our community.

Guest Reflection

I didn't believe I was beautiful growing up. My husband, who at that time was my boyfriend, was the one whom I remember first called me beautiful. I didn't see myself as beautiful. I had skin burns on my feet and I thought since it was hard for everyone to look at it, that it didn't make me beautiful. When he accepted them and didn't care, I started to not care either. I always had a problem with the length of my hair however. I was always trying to put it in a pony-tail since the age I could remember and remembering not being satisfied with it because it was dingy. Every black girl's problem is that they may not feel like they are beautiful because they don't have long flowing hair like a white girl. I believed that too. When I first got my perm, I was in heaven. I could shake my head and my hair would move like a white girl, so I thought I was the bomb. But that didn't last because I had to take care of my hair. When I didn't keep up with it, it started breaking off. Then when I was in middle school I got a weave. At that time, you had to glue it in and boy, nobody could tell me anything. I thought I was everything. Then after a while the weave got shabby and that no longer looked hot. So, my mother asked me if I wanted to grow locks. She encouraged me to get them by saying that my hair would grow all the way down to my back by the time I was in high school. With that said, I was on board. I started locking my hair in middle school, but they didn't tell me I had to cut out the perm in order to start and by the time they cut out the perm, I had a very short afro. I thought I looked like a boy and I had to go back to school! My mom bought me these cheap earrings and a stretchy head band so that I could look feminine. It didn't matter because that same year The Nutty Professor came out which was the worse because locks weren't a trend at that time and they called them "***t-locks" for my remaining years in middle school into high school. Out of all my other schools, moving to this predominantly black area during high school with majority blacks had me being teased the worse I've ever been before. I've never experienced it so bad. So, at that time, I just didn't care anymore. My mom no longer bought me clothes after middle school. I became a tom-boy and started acting out in school. Smoking, drinking and getting in trouble until I had a boyfriend, then you couldn't tell me anything. I started doing better in school and basically, he got me through high school financially. He bought me everything. When he bought sneakers, I got sneakers. It was great. I had to develop confidence on my own and realize that it didn't come from all of these magazines out here and guys telling me that I'm beautiful and what not. I had to know that I believed I was beautiful whether you told me or not. I like my natural hair and I keep myself clean. Having good hygiene is what I considered was beautiful because it was what I could control.

- Age 31

Journal Entry

What up Shelly!

How you doin' girl?! Sike, I know how you doing cause you doing my hair right now. Anyway, I got mad stuff to tell you about my conversation with Dante before he left for his vacation. First, when I got online I wasn't talkin' to him because of what Rashaun told me and how people be saying he be talkin' ish about me behind my back. But he instant messaged me first talking about let me say wassup to you before we don't talk to each other anymore, so I was like hi or whatever. We were talkin' for a while and then he was like, so are we still on for the prom or whatever (cause since I'm going to another school next year when we were still talking, he said we would be going to the prom together even if we broke up between now and our senior year). I said I don't know now because you seem two faced to me. I said that to him and I was like cause you seem to be all nice and ish to me in person but people tell me you talk mad ish behind my back. He was like who you hear this bull from now and of course he blamed it on Jamiah and Antoine because that's who usually tells me ish about him. I was like no it was Rashaun. Ha! I blamed it on your man! Anyway, he was like Rashaun should talk, he's playin' Shelby or some ish like that. I was like how the hell is he playin' Shelby, he don't even go out with her. He kept talking more stuff and defended himself of course but I kinda believe him though. I know you probably think I'm in denial though... but if you only saw the things he wrote. D@&$-it! I can't believe I deleted this ish. I don't know, but after that we weren't fighting anymore and he was like you know what I'm going to miss you Stephy cause you was f' it, you IS special to me. He *said those exact words I swear. I believe him of course. I was like awwwww.... then I said I'm sorry that I caused you so much stress and all this stuff I apologized for. I forget. Anyways, he was like it's aight because without the stress we wouldn't be as special to each other because it's special how long we stayed together even though we had so many fights. He was still tryin' to kick game after that trying to get with me but then I was like no because I would hear too much ish from my friends so he was like "true" and stuff. He was like I'm really gonna miss you Steph and stuff like that and I was like awwww I'm gonna miss you too. We probably said a lot more but then he was like, you still want your necklace? I was like hold up, what necklace? He was like I bought it for you and I was gonna give you it the Friday before I left. I was like stop playing!!! Really bold big and ish. He kept on saying it and I kept saying stop playin'. He was like I ain't playin and I was like you serious and he was like yeah d@&$-it. He was like sorry after that for saying that but he really did buy it. He was like it was a gold chain with a heart and an "S" on it. I was like awwwww. I remember when he asked me like before when we went out he asked me if I wanted anything and I was like nahh of course, don't buy anything. (You know how I am). He was like nah. I want to buy you something so he was like how about jewelry. No, SIKE yea... I think I said that back. Anyway, but you know how I say sike when I was really serious but then he was like nah what kinda jewelry? I was like how about a chain with a heart on the end or maybe an "S". I guess he remembered and got me it. He said he told me he was gonna get it sooner or later. I was like awwww for real. I don't care if you don't believe me but I believe him. If you* *just saw all the stuff he writes. I know I left mad stuff out that he said to me too, but I believe him until I tell you guys what he says... well mostly Katrina and Jamiah because they always have something negative to say about it. That's why I don't want them to know about me and Dante's conversation. That's why I like to tell you more. Anyways, you don't know how mad I am that I deleted our conversation. Then you would believe me more. Oh well, I know I left mad parts out. This is just a brief description. So what's up with you and Rashaun? It's your turn to ramble on about your life story. I already took up five f'in' pages so here's my closing. TTYL (Talk To You Later is what that means).*

Your friend,

Stephanie

PS. Sorry so sloppy, I'll make it neater next time

CHAPTER 2
IN SPITE OF... LOVE YOURSELF!

Finding the beauty within can become challenging if you're not able to like who you are first. And where does that come from exactly? According to the NJ Family magazine article "Raising Resilient Kids", that researches the 5 ways to foster strength and character and proves to be the single best predictor of a child's emotional health and happiness, professor Robyn Fivush and Duke studied how the impact of advancing a family narrative, making a point of telling stories to your children of your family's shared history- creates stronger kids. And their research is demonstrating that this is indeed a key factor. No wonder why many of the folklore or children narrative books that we read growing up most often had elders from all cultures showing a sense of pride, honor, and tradition. Stories would be told while the young were sitting in various circles at their elder's feet, listening to the stories of the brave men and women that came before them and the adventures they were able to experience in their lives. These stories and adventures gave wonderful heroes to look up to and learn from. Duke continues:

...there are people who faced the worse and made it through. And this sense of continuity and relatedness seem to serve the purpose in kids of making them more resilient.

Ordinary families can be special because they each have a

history no other family has. They all have Uncle So and So, they all have Aunt So and So. They all have a brother who went off and did this adventure and everyone has a story that no one else has. So, if you know that, it makes you special, it's a fingerprint.

NY Times columnist Bruce Feiler came up with similar findings as well which was, adapted from his book, The Secrets of Happy Families; How to Improve Your Morning, Rethink Family Dinner, Fight Smart, Go Out and Play, and Much More, and after a while a surprising theme emerged; "The single most important thing you can do for your family is develop a strong family narrative." (Grover, 2013)

We understand that we are all challenged from one time or another with the scrutiny we receive based on our outside appearances. But how can you learn to love yourself and find the beauty within, when you can't even embrace who you truly are and where you have originally come from? How can you truly love yourself when you're trying to be something other than what you actually are, based on some random standards, someone else's, society, or what yourself thinks you should be? I believe the first step of finding the beauty within is accepting where you originally came from, as research has suggested. Knowing your family history and the stories, good and bad, that close family members, relatives and ancestors have gone through, gives you a sense of identity and pride in oneself and an ancestry line that no one else has. Although thus far, throughout this book I have focused on the plight of blacks in America throughout the years, I find it necessary for everyone to embrace their heritage as one sense of self and identity. Truly, beginning to identify and love the place and history your family and ancestors originated proves to be one of the better solutions in building both your family and children up into being better people. I admire the sense of pride someone is able to have as they acknowledge the island, country or culture that they belong to and actually know the roots and past history of their family as something they are a part of and can take pride in. Unfortunately for many blacks of America, this history has been uprooted from us due to the deliberate and debilitating process that slave masters perpetuated in order to strip that history from us for the very reasons we see today. We were kept from understanding who and where we came from, resulting in us not having a sense of pride of where we originated as this article so poignantly points out. These things were needed in order to build stronger and more emotionally healthy and resilient kids.

What sense of self can you establish after years and years of being stripped, pulled on and beaten down? Eventually, this type of pressure is going to have you losing some sense of pride, right? I beg to differ! Many cultures have had a history of being the oppressed and down trodden. However, what distinguishes some from others is not the remembering of that part of history about their ancestors that was glossed over and never revisited, but it is the constant story-telling and remembering of distinct facts that took place regularly, that influences the up-bringing of children, families and communities. Ray Jasper said it best in A Letter from Ray Jasper Who is About to Be Executed: Postcards from the Edge taken from Nolan Hamilton, before being executed in Texas (2014). "It's really an epidemic, the number of blacks locked up in this country; that's why I look, not only at my own situation, but why all of us young blacks are in prison. I've come to see, it's largely due to an identity crisis. We don t know our history. We don't know how to really identify with white people. We are really of a different culture, but by being slaves, we lost ourselves." He goes on to say what he believes would help blacks be more accepting of their identity:

Black history shouldn't be a month, it should be a course, an elective taught year-round. I guarantee black kids would take that course if it was available to them. How many black kids would change their outlook if they knew that they were only considered 3/5's of a human being according to the U.S Constitution? That black people were considered part animal in this country. They don't know that. When you learn that, you carry yourself with a different level of dignity for all we've overcome.

Before Martin Luther King was killed he drafted a bill called 'The Bill for the Disadvantaged'. It was for blacks and poor whites. King understood that in order to have a successful life, you have to decrease the odds of failure. You have to change the playing field. I'm not saying there's no personal responsibility for success. That goes without saying, but there's also a corporate responsibility.

I think we've all been waiting for the government and successful businesses and congressmen to take a corporate responsibility way too long that is slowly chipping away at the disadvantages for a large group of people (In some cases). However, when it comes to the upbringing of our own, I believe that we ourselves have to take more responsibility in instilling the values and positive self-images that we want our youth to have as a whole. Therefore, as Ray has so directly stated, I believe seeking as many personal stories as we can from the family elders who are accessible and willing to tell and gaining knowledge by reading books, attending historical venues and educating ourselves as well as our children will enlighten us about our history and will instill a sense of pride for one's self-worth. That means, elders, you must tell the stories and that means everyone, PAY ATTENTION to the stories that you are being told and learn from them!

I remember my grandmother visiting us often from VA during the summer months around her birthday. That was during my early years in college. At this time, as for most college students, I was even more aware of who I was and getting to know what I was going to become as I struggled to survive this make-you-or-break-you process. I knew my goal was to become a more responsible adult and to make it on my own. However independent I was or thought I was at this time, I began to have this intense longing to know my background and I wanted to explore my history further and how we overall connected to the greater scheme of things that happened in our world.

I know my grandmother at some time in her life, lived in North Carolina as well as my grandfather who she later married. My parents were both from Virginia, but neither really talked about their experiences growing up at a time when segregation was very real and prominent in the South when my parents were children and teenagers. I would at times muster up the courage to ask my grandmother about her experiences as we began to draw quite close in my later years. Since she lived so far away and we didn't get to see each other much except on special holidays, I didn't have a lot of time to converse with her. However, grandma wasn't as eager to share the history of our ancestors or the stories of our family and sort of skirted the questions, or acknowledged them as passing thoughts.

Other family members thought about some of these questions but left my questions unanswered as if they were rhetorical ones. Unfortunately, I did not persist or pursue my eagerness to know, so eventually I left it alone until recently when my grandmother was around 92. Talking or remembering had become more of a challenge and a task to get her to open up about our family history. However, this time she was much more willing and ready to put out the information. Good, bad and indifferent, no matter how gruesome the facts were, they were great to hear and helped explain why our family makeup was the way it was and why certain things had taken place in our lives. It gave me a renewed sense of self and I was satisfied knowing some, any or whatever they may have been so that I could feel closer to where my family has been.

That explains why Dr. Duke and Fivush's research (2013) stated that "The more children knew about their family's history, the stronger their sense of control over their lives, the higher their self-esteem, and the more successful they believed their families functioned." I believe this is why Ray believes there is an influx of blacks in jail. "Young blacks need to learn their identity so they can have more respect for the blacks that suffered for their liberties than they have for someone talking about selling drugs over a rap beat who really isn't selling drugs." The Drs. concluded that children who have the most self-confidence have what they call a "strong intergenerational-self". They know they belong to something positive that was bigger than them. This can be daunting however, if you have very little to no contact with your family and the history thereof.

Our Initial Family

In that case if you are questioning your worth and identity there is however, one overall Creator who has given us all the best sense of self and identity that we could ever ask for. Understanding that God is our Creator and maker helps us to know who we are as a child of the one and only maker. It may be hard for some to grasp that this is true. However, how many of us have a hard time because we feel like we don't belong or fit in anywhere; or we are trying so hard to fit in and belong somewhere and find ourselves trying to measure up in some way or another, only to eventually feel rejected? Or we may measure up and feel accepted according to the standards of everyone around us, but we find ourselves depressed because we're trying to be someone we aren't and not who we were originally created to be. That's because we often times are trying to find our sense of self through others around us and not already knowing that something or someone much better has already accepted us and that is God himself. The only validation that we all truly need is from Him and He has already told us in His word that He "created mankind in his own image, in the image of God he created them; male and female" Genesis 1:27. He also tells us that "We are fearfully and wonderfully made" Psalm 139:14. You can't be more accepted by anyone than that! God is the only one who knows how many hairs are on your head! Who else knows these intricate details about you but Him!

If God, the ruler over everyone in the entire universe said I am made in His image, that's all the validation and acceptance that I truly need. No one can ever again make me feel less than who I really am as a black, brown-skinned, skinny and short mother and wife who had a daughter out of wedlock, because God already justified me and accepted me as his own. Although these may be pejoratives that others may place on me, I can stand proudly and confidently knowing that I am still a child of God and lovingly accepted by him nevertheless. Unfortunately, it's still not always so easy to accept yourself even though you know this to be the truth. It can be constantly challenged in many occasions as the enemy always tries to whisper lies about your true self-worth and value to God. (Especially if you make a mistake) However, make a declaration on a regular and daily basis to Be All Whom God Called You to Be regardless of what others expect OR you may expect from yourself. The truth always remains that God loves you and accepts you for who you are so continuously remain in that most comforting state of peace and security. Then you can start understanding and realizing your beauty within because you'll be finding your identity in Christ and not in the outside influences that fabricate what beauty really is.

Guest Reflection

Males perception of beauty is all screwed up also. Me and my friends would go after the Spanish girls because of the videos; Rap videos. It took me a while to get out of that understanding. I believe it comes from who you surround yourself with; your social circle. The media plays a huge part on what males think they should go after and which group of women is more appealing.

I lived in subsidized housing. Drug Infiltrated. Heavy drugs. Although I grew up in Westfield which is a predominantly affluent and white city, there was a neighborhood in Westfield where it was all black. As a child I saw people doing drugs. I saw people being chased by the police all throughout my neighborhood.

My mother didn't graduate high school and had me

when she was 16. I am one of six children. She never pushed us in school. I don't think she knew how.

When you don't have a good relationship with your mother, you blame a lot of things on your mother. She would stay out of the house hours at a time.

My grandmother tried to keep my confidence up. My mom didn't. The insecurities came from the people around me. My siblings always made fun of how light I was or how big my head was. To me I didn't deal with it that well. That combined with school didn't allow me to have the confidence I needed to do as well as I think I could have done. I always wanted to be dark skinned because I didn't want to stand out. If you were lighter, you were supposed to be liked by white people but that was never my experience.

In school, I felt inferior because even when I tried, I still felt like I would fail. I have two experiences I'll never forget in school. In 3rd grade, the teacher came up to two of the only black students in class to ask us if we were uncomfortable after she read something in regards to black history month in front of the entire class. The one month they acknowledge the things black people did in US history.

It played a big part on my self-confidence. I never wanted to be singled out. Going to an all-white school, I never wanted to stand out. I always wanted to blend in. I struggled with reading. Whenever I was called on in class to read even into high school I always felt inferior and would get really hot and nervous.

They always told me how bad I was doing. In my grade, I was the only black male who wasn't in special education. I was in a big class and I was the only black person. I always felt dumber than everyone because they were getting the good grades and I was always getting average grades. I felt as though they had everything and were doing better than me so that means they must be smart and I was in the same class getting average grades so that made me stupid.

I always knew I didn't have as much as they had. I got free lunch. The milk was nasty, the peanut butter sandwiches were smooshed in the plastic bags and the sandwiches tasted like plastic. I would always ask them if they wanted the left-over food on their plate because the other food tasted better. What we got for lunch was disgusting.

Another incident I remember in 3rd grade is when the teacher told me he was going to call to tell me what I had to do for my project. But I remember distinctly that I told him he couldn't because we didn't have a phone. We really didn't have one.

The worst experience when my identity was attacked however, was when I was younger, and the older people were making fun of me. These are the people I'm surrounded with. I didn't really hang around people my age. So, I kind of just laughed it off because everyone else was laughing at me. I didn't really get made fun of at school, it was my inside circle and neighborhood. It hurt me. It affected me because I wasn't getting self-esteem from anyone else. If it wasn't head jokes, it was jokes about my clothes. That's another thing that we do to each other. If you don't walk out with name brand shoes or whatever is hot at that time. You look at yourself like I NEED TO TAKE THIS OFF and throw it away when I get home. My mother embedded that in me from a young age.

Later after reading several writings that black scholars wrote I realized that it is called a Reflection. When you say something about someone else, that's really how you feel about yourself.

So, I didn't develop a true love for myself until after college. Black scholars overall gave me insight on what this world is really about and the tactics that they use to get you to think a certain way, act a certain way. It blew my mind.

My father was successful in his career as an engineer. I would lie to my father when he called about how I was doing. He wasn't around, and his career pushed him farther away from his kids. He was career driven so the people that me and my friends hung around with saw basketball players and rappers as successful.

I became rebellious in high school, but basketball became my passion and kept me focused and staying on the right path. When basketball season was around, I would be on time for school, all of my homework was done, and I was doing well in everything. As soon as basketball season was over, I was right back doing what I wanted to do with no direction or focus. Getting into whatever, I wanted to get myself into.

My friends and I talked about sports and the latest rap videos. To talk about anything else, you would be considered an outcast.

My brother, friend and I were the only ones who went to college – out of us 3 only 2 graduated from college. This is within a 30-year span amongst the males within my neighborhood! For the females it is definitely different.

Now, I have a passion to understand more about where I come from since I have been stripped from it for so long. School hasn't prepared you enough for college.

I never considered my mother to be beautiful until I believed I looked good. After college when I started diving into our history I learned to love my history and found even a little bit of history about my family lineage. It definitely boosted my confidence and I realize now that I am the best. I didn't do the best in college because I didn't know that I could do my best.

Because of boredom I remember my friends and I thought about robbing in Central Ave. Fortunately I didn't do it and it kept me from falling victim to the system until I was convicted for 9 years as an adult because someone from my neighborhood charged me after an altercation during a basketball fight. I couldn't work while I was in college because of my record.

My step brother (father's son) grew up in a very affluent part of DC and hung around a lot of white boys. Because of his social circle he now dates a lot of white girls. I believe a lot of black men think this is better since it was considered unattainable for some. Therefore, those men who do get a good job or a high degree feel like they are supposed to date white women now because they have gained some sort of prestige.

But after I read Francis Cress Welsing and once I tapped into the psyche, I connected all the dots. She was saying the darker you are the more of a threat you are.

Now I believe, if you are a woman and wear your natural hair I think it is beautiful. It shows that you're comfortable with how you look and you're not trying to look like anyone else. Women who put weave in their younger daughter's hair are teaching them to self-hate. It shows me that you're able to embrace who you are when you wear your own hair and now I just say thank you. I now look for it.

That's not the case for all men though. I know a dark skinned beautiful girl who cut off all of her hair and none of my friends liked it. I loved it and was able to appreciate her natural beauty.

But I encourage all young men and women to EMBRACE WHO YOU ARE. You are perfect. There's nothing wrong with you. There is something wrong with you if you want to look like something that is not you.

Embrace yourself and how you look.

With the media, period. I believe that there's always a hidden agenda. I always felt like Lupita Nyong'o was beautiful and I don't need you to approve it for me. I'm sure the media wouldn't consider another one like her beautiful in another incident, so I'm confused.

-   Age 27

CHAPTER 3
JUST CUT IT OFF AND LET YOUR LIGHT SHINE THROUGH!

"Uhhh! I'm just so tired of this hair! I want to go natural but I don't know the proper ways in doing it." "How about you just chop it off? You have the face for it" says a well-meaning beautician.

Well there it is. Without much thought about it at all, I decided to start my natural hair process from scratch and shave off all my hair! What a big and bold statement that was to the world! I was either a feminist, world activist, going through something or just plain crazy! More likely the latter two but what a statement and how freeing it was to not have to worry about my hair. The first time I decided to shave it all off, it was probably due to more laziness than anything since I didn't feel like putting so much emphasis on my hair. The Battles of the Hair was finally over; Over with my mom, over with the world, over with myself. Finally, I could wake up, get dressed and not have to worry about the intrusive comments from my outside world about my hair. Or did I? Of course, I did! Why would I ever think that was likely to happen? Shaving your head was a huge statement that was bound to draw even more attention than before. However, surprisingly more often than not, I received a lot of positive feedback. Now, since my face was more presently visible, many positive comments came back in regard to having no hair! What is that about? What gives? I should have shaved my hair a long time ago! My issues with hair would have been minute to non-existent! I take that back. Kids can be cruel and unfortunately due to the constant pressures and victimization that some cultures or people in general have to go through in regard to their skin color, hair texture, nationality and so forth, the adolescents that are often privy and bombarded by these blatant yet "subtle" messages of what beauty is reflect their perceived knowledge on each other and most unfortunately on themselves.

How then does one come to grow up into developing their own sense of beauty, where these images and normal ways of understanding of beauty no longer exist? Is there in fact such a thing where people are able to effectively displace themselves from the institutionalized views that surround them without truly thinking this is what is beautiful, and this is what isn't? We all want to not own up to our respective shallowness that has developed very early on in our developmental process. However, are we being true to ourselves when we sincerely desire to look at the inward man first before deciding someone's aesthetics as being highly attractive and favorable in the eyes of the beholder?

This takes me to my first experiences of looking beyond the surface. First, we have to understand what surface truly is. Surface as described in the Merriam-Webster's dictionary states that it is 1) anything on the outside of a body or object. 2) outward aspect or appearance.

I can look at a picture of our beautiful daughter Mya. She took gorgeous pictures when I was pursuing her career in acting. In this picture her skin is glowing with her big, bright beautiful eyes, beautiful black hair and innocent Cheshire cat smile. (I love her smile and her almond shaped eyes) Yet, as any eight-year-old can, she can put on a huge facade when in public, yet when she gets home her moody and disrespectful character could come out with a flip of a switch. (Man, I wonder where she gets that from?) She watches everything! People, singers, dancers, actors, animals and could do an impression of them that would have you on the floor by the rolling of the eyes, head and sucking teeth that she so poignantly emulates. If you didn't know her truthfully, she could fool you by the innocence she displays at first glance. However, we know as eight-year-olds we are ever so developing our inner character. Our sense of what is right and what is wrong on so many levels; who to hang out with vs. whom not to because of values. All of these are outside factors that have to do with the up building or tearing down of our inner character.

Now as we have already stated, God is more concerned with our inner character qualities, "Our hidden man of the heart, the quiet and meek spirit within." How many can attest that that's what we truly look at when we first take a glimpse at a picture on the cover of a magazine or a photo on Facebook? How often are we so readily able to see someone's inner man rather than the surface appearance that is first shown us? I can attest that it can be extremely hard. Often times we rely on what has been developed within us from a young age to determine someone's worth rather than someone's heart. Unfortunately, these ideas of how we view people are developed within us at the adolescent age and at times are extremely hard to shake.

Does your surface affect your character? I remember when I first decided to stop dressing a certain way. I had to think about what image I was portraying as I decided to be more committed in my relationship to Christ. Yet how I was dressing wasn't a direct reflection to what I was displaying in my everyday lifestyle. Something had to change. Understanding who I was in Christ made me realize that maybe my shape didn't have to be so obviously displayed to the surrounding world. There are some things that just don't have to be shared. Therefore, I decided to no longer wear a certain type of jean and to find a style to fit more of my personality which was wearing more dresses that were flattering to my shape.

Luckily, my god-sister was having a yard sale and asked me if I had any clothes that I wanted to give away. I practically gave away everything; Brand new fitted jeans, tops that may have been a little more provocative because of the see-through material. Also, I gave away my tiny little shorts and high-heel shoes. Some may be intentionally thinking that you should not feel obligated to wear certain types of clothes in order to be one committed to Christ or the like. Even though He does say "Whose adorning let it not be that outward adorning of plaiting the hair, and of wearing of gold, or of putting on of apparel; But let it be the hidden man of the heart, in that which is not corruptible, even the ornament of a meek and quiet spirit, which is in the sight of God of great price", you still should have some freedom in displaying who you are as a child of God without looking like a nun in a convent, right?

How many of us decide not to put on something that in some form or fashion doesn't reflect who we are? Many of us do. Just because something is trendy at the moment doesn't necessarily mean that it's for me. What we wear shouldn't define solely who we are altogether, but you have the ability to decide what or what you're not going to wear based on who you are and on what you stand. Therefore, what you stand for should determine how you want to carry yourself, which aligns with what kind of message you are sending to the rest of the world. Your attire does play a part. It shouldn't overshadow your character, but it should reflect who and what you represent. It can be a distraction and false signal to others on what or whom you are truly representing which can obscure the overall message you are sending to the rest of the world.

With that said, I believe that this type of surface beauty is different than the beauty you are born with. The facial features, color of your skin and the like is the type of surface that you embrace and live with for the rest of your life. Complicating it with surgical procedures, skin creams and added expenditures doesn't change who you are so why even bother? It takes away from the creativity that God extended to you as His own. Why try and alter the beautiful creation that He already made you to be when He already calls you His own? It's our unwillingness to accept the fact that He made us this way in totality and our inability to embrace every uniqueness and perfection that He has created us to be. We only call them imperfections because of the standards that we measure ourselves up to in our society. It is time that we give up trying to be like everyone else and start being satisfied with ourselves as a whole; Without the weaves, without the false breasts, without the nose job, without the colored hair. Loving others starts with loving ourselves as we take care of our temples (our bodies) first by being able to embrace God's unconditional love for who HE made us to be. Thank God, He loves us just the way He made us. Finding the beauty within, first, without all of the expenditures, should be the only thing you need to have the confidence to be yourself. Then whether you have these things on or not, you will already know who you are and that you are beautiful all by yourself because your true beauty comes from understanding who you are in Christ! Nothing more and nothing less.

So, what were my findings as I decided to change the way I dressed and focus more on my inner character? Unfortunately, yet fortunately I discovered that my character was jacked way up to the tenth degree! It was not so readily revealed to me at first since the reasons I was doing this in the first place was an honest attempt to draw closer to God. I believed not focusing so much on my outer appearance would align me more with putting more focus on what God wanted me to do and be. Indeed, it did. I was so much more conscious of what I believed God wanted me to do that developed a ready heart to serve and Be All God Called me to be and called me to do. I wanted to tell everyone about God's goodness. I wanted to use my gift the way God intended me to use it and grow. I was a part of every ministry that my heart so desired, while trying to hold a full-time teaching job and being a single mother to a child under the age of 6. You can imagine the young lady running around doing everything, trying to be everywhere and in everything like a" turkey with its head cut off". Although God may have given me some successes in seeing Him work through all the things I was trying to accomplish in my life, I realize now that He had more order for me. He wanted to give me more peace and more of a focus that was in line with how He created me and wanted me to be. I was so busy trying to do, do, do for Him that my focus soon became doing to get a reward instead of living intentionally through the word. I realize now that it wasn't so much what I said to others as much as it was what was said through the life that I was living.

Oh, what a beautiful life I thought I was living. I received my undergrad and Master's while having a child, traveling back and forth to New York and working full-time! I was also a leader of a ministry and had such a zeal for the Lord! Yet all that I was accomplishing at a fairly young age, I believe, still didn't deal with the inner, inner heart and deep hidden motives that led me to this place of doing so much in the first place. God wanted to work on the core of my heart and the inner bitterness, anger and resentment that took place prior to all of this running around that got me here in the first place. He was now ready to work on my character, my inner woman in ways that brought me to tears as I unveiled the truth to why it was so hard for me to be still in the first place. Things that I experienced from childhood that I had no idea impacted the way I looked at myself and the lack of confidence that I had and had to eventually develop. I had to evaluate, understand and dismantle wrong thinking as time went on so I would no longer respond to situations in the same manner.

Realizing all of these things allowed me to have time to take a step back and examine my inner heart's motives, and the jealousy, selfishness, and envy that I had to learn to overcome when I realized my true beauty within and the uniqueness that I possessed. However, it wasn't until I decided to take time to realign my focus on what God saw anyway. At first, I covered myself with whatever outer cosmetics, cute outfits, shoes or perfume that you almost feel obligated to wear according to worldly standards. Now, however, I was able to focus on the confidence I had through Him and Him alone. No longer did the outward appearance that I was eventually able to find some satisfaction in, give me my identity. It was the boldness and assurance of who I was in Christ that began to shape and mold me into the assurance of who I was. As I continued to study God's word and move in obedience, I saw the work He was doing in my life. Although my appearance at times would be verbally attacked due to my now carelessness in keeping up my outward appearance or making sure my apparel was up to date or even groomed altogether, those comments didn't faze me. My focus was so heavy handed on the spiritual and keeping up with what I believed God wanted me to keep my focus on, that I totally began to lose that interest of what I even looked like on the outside. I had to have some common decency however only for the sake of being well put together as I represented the school and kids in which I worked.

However, any form of going above and beyond I began to look at as worldly and unimportant. Soon I also formed a sense of haughtiness and pride that slowly but surely began to rise up as an additional negative characteristic that God now had to deal with to tweak my character. My new focus eventually developed into a religious and judgmental attitude about others that still didn't allow me to focus on the real heart of the matter. I thought that since I was "behaving" in the sense of not doing those things that I deemed so highly as sinful (sex), I was doing extremely well. However, God had to show me that it had nothing to do with what I wore on my outer surface or the way he carefully designed me to look. When that was no longer a focus it didn't matter that I was now so religious and "holier than thou" either. The truth and beauty of it all is what came from within. The Bible explains it further in

Luke 18: 10-14. Jesus gives us a parable comparing a Pharisee and a publican to show us what is most important to him. It begins with two men going into the temple to pray. One man says "God, I thank thee, that I am not as other men are, extortioners, unjust, adulterers, or even as this publican. I fast twice in the week; I give tithes of all that I possess." Yet, the other man humbly prays "God be merciful to me a sinner". In the end we realize that the humble publican's prayer was more acceptable than the boastful and self-righteous Pharisee's.

Jesus was meek and humble. He didn't exalt himself amongst the people that he healed and ministered to. More often than not, he told everyone that he healed to tell no one what had happened, or to declare what God had done for them. God always did the exalting of his son while he was on earth. Jesus stayed meek, humble and under the radar unless he was called on to do otherwise by His father in Heaven. He had a loving spirit full of compassion for the people in need. Not a haughty and boisterous spirit that declared "HERE I AM!" "LOOK AT ME AND THE GREAT THINGS I'M DOING!" That is what He wanted me to get. I had to learn how to truly love. Truly forgive and be patient with others and myself. Truly let go of who hurt me, what hurt me, how I hurt myself and others that continuously had me looking back and replaying the things that I did in my life to affect my present state. I had to learn to speak the truth and be transparent. Not condemning, unforgiving and hypocritical. God wanted me to be able to speak from a real place so that others could also learn to be real to themselves. Consequently, I could truly move on and LIVE! After God was able to deal with me in these areas, I was able to truly see my beauty within and tap into the power that God wanted me to embrace and realize that He created this in me from the very beginning!!

So, who are you? Truly? Not your job or your status in this world? Who are you? What are your likes and dislikes? What are the complex situations that took place in your life that make you who you are today? Were you willing and able to forgive those who needed to be forgiven or are you still dealing with the bitterness of past hurts from someone you are still unable to forgive even today? Were you never called beautiful by the very ones who you expected to acknowledge you as so? Or were you in turn called beautiful so much by others but were unable to accept it for yourself because of the experiences and challenges you had to go through in life? When you look in the mirror who do you really see? Hopefully not an imposter, but one who God really created you to be in your own right. Not what you want others to think that you think about yourself. What do you really see? What is the truth behind the mask that you may be constantly putting on every day and night as you face the world maybe unconsciously waiting for their acceptance?

Know this, that the Father accepts you and knows exactly who you are and who He created you to be. So, don't be afraid to explore more of what that means to you.

It's probably time for you to really embrace the beauty within and consciously identify the habits, kinks, idiosyncrasies, judgments, mishaps and the like that God so desires for you to research. Sometimes it can be so deeply embedded in you it seems totally out of your control. Sometimes the idiosyncrasies, mishaps and judgments were placed on you from generations before you. You realize that some of the challenges you go through have been experienced by your mother, father, aunts, uncles, or grandparents before you. That's why it's so crucial to know and accept the history of your family. Sometimes what you do and why you do what you do is beyond your control or were habits placed on you by generations before you that needed to be broken. I invite you to explore them further and understand them better for your own sake, so that you will no longer continue to move in and accept them as your own. Consciously unveil them and admit what they are so you can rightfully expose them and in turn deal with them, so they can be dealt with and become no more!

I know as a black nation we have many preconceived notions about what beautiful is because of what was ingrained in us. Many of us have experienced being the "black sheep" or perceived ourselves as the outcasts of the family. That may have affected your sense of worth and acceptance. Those ideologies and understandings of who is considered inferior to the world, compared to who should be of a higher status, sadly still permeates through our world today. Hate is still out there, whether we want to admit it or not, because of the shade of our skin and the experiences we have had and had to live through. These all need to be dealt with in a real and mature manner. No one can or should make you feel less than you feel you are if you don't feel that way about yourself first. If you endured put downs by people who were of authority over you, those are situations and experiences that need to be addressed. You can't pretend that those words didn't affect you because we all know that words do hurt most of the time if not always. If you didn't consciously deal with that hurt at the initial time it occurred, you most likely could have taken them to heart and it could have negatively affected your perception of yourself.

If you were never told constantly that you were beautiful from your father or the men in your life, and believed it, and in turn found yourself seeking attention from men in places that you knew was detrimental to you, those feelings and experiences need to be dealt with. Forgiveness of whomever you considered the guilty parties of this neglect needs to take place. Forgiveness of you for consciously or unconsciously looking for a way to feel good about yourself outside of yourself needs to be meaningfully addressed and dealt with also. Sometimes you do have to take a "Selah" (pause; and think about it) moment in order to gather yourself and move on with the best self that you want and need to be. Doing so much and constantly moving isn't going to help you to get to the better you. The beauty within that needs to come out as you stop, reflect, dismantle and grow to your fullest potential only will come with some sort of stillness. It feels great to hear my father say, "You look nice today" or that "You're beautiful". It sounds AMAZING when my husband acknowledges me as "The most beautiful woman in his eyes." However, there's nothing better than knowing that you feel that way TRULY about yourself first. You may not think that you're the most beautiful woman in the world, because you understand the importance of not comparing yourself as better or less than anyone else, but you can honestly stand in the mirror and love what you see without all the added expenditures. Knowing that you're a child of God and that He loves you will help you to grow from within, so that whatever shines within can expand to whatever is seen on the outer you. This is a revelation everyone should have and experience.

Solange Knowles explained it best when she made her debut on Oprah's show with the big chopping of her hair. She knew for herself that she felt not as beautiful or widely accepted when she didn't have a weave in her hair. She described this to be "bondage" or "submission" to this ideal that weave in some form or fashion made her look better than what she would have looked like without it. I regard this as a truth for most women who succumb to the wearing of weave for whatever reasons. I don't have anything against weave, per se, but what I do not think is healthy, especially for women of African descent is our thinking that this type of hair makes me look better and prettier than I would look if I was to not have it. In some sort of way, it is denouncing the person's ability to find the original beauty that God has blessed them with. In some shape or form viewing one style as the quintessential expression of what beauty is has everyone in some form or fashion looking like everyone else, which is why I believe, as well as the remaining audience that saw Solange come out that day with her big chop, the beauty that she was created to be. No one else walks, talks and looks like her and her hair was a replica of how God originally created her hair to look like. I believe Chris Rock said it best when he stated, "You don't look like everyone else (the average chic), now we can see you".

Metamorphosis vs. Masquerade

The metamorphosis or masqueraded transformation is how it is explained according to Romans 12:1, 2 and 2 Corinthians 3:18, that Warren W. Wiersbe discusses in the book Real Worship; It Will Transform Your Life. According to Wiersbe, Paul contrasts two ways of life in these scriptures; that of the believer that is transformed by God, and that of the believer who is transformed for the world.

I beseech you therefore, brethren, by the mercies of God, that you present your bodies a living sacrifice, holy, acceptable to God, which is your reasonable service. And do not be conformed to this world, but be transformed by the renewing of your mind, that you may prove what is that good and acceptable and perfect will of God.

~Romans 12:1, 2

But we all, with unveiled face, beholding as in a mirror the glory of the Lord, are being transformed into the same image from glory to glory, just as by the Spirit of the Lord.

~ 2 Corinthians 3:18

Wiersbe explains this contrast as a "contrast between metamorphosis and masquerade. The 'transformer' lives by power from within, but the 'conformer' lives by the pressure from without". He goes on to explain, using a paraphrase by J.P. Phillips, "Don't let the world around you squeeze you into its own mold, but let God remake you so that your attitude of mind is changed."

It's like the beautiful butterfly that emerges out of the cocoon that we marvel at how transformed this tiny, little creature can become. The metamorphosis of this creature allowed it "to be changed into another form" but this change comes from within. "The change that happened on the outside is the normal and natural expression of the nature on the inside."(Wiersbe, 1986) As believers you should want to be changed into another form different than what this world has to offer. Dare to be you. Stand up and stand out as the infamous Tye Tribett used to sing, "Be not conformed to this world!"

However, there is another Greek word that Wiersbe used, metaschendataconia, and it is usually translated "fashioned" or "conformed". When you conform to this world and fashion your life after the pattern of people who are of this world, you are changing the outside, but your change is not coming from within. "The first thing Jesus said was clean up your behavior, not just your façade".

More specifically He said, "You Pharisees clean the outside of the cup and dish, but inside you are full of greed and wickedness". It is not metamorphosis if you are still trying to be a Christian but living worldly. It is a masquerade when you allow your conformation to overtake you. That goes for worldly conformation as well as religious conformation. The Pharisees had learned how to do the external things well- the rituals, and traditions everyone could see. However, the externals were just a masquerade to keep people from looking at the person's true character, whether they really had love in their hearts or not.

Let us instead strive for the example of Christs' transfiguration on the mount which describes the metamorphosis, "as His face shone like the son, and His clothes became white as the light". He was able to show the disciples the glory of God that was within Him, "radiating in shadow-less splendor". The apostle John wrote "And we behold His glory, the glory as of the only begotten of the Father, full of grace and truth", John 1:14.

When Jesus' glory was revealed, it was not a masquerade. The glory that he possessed on the inside came from within and transformed to whatever pure, overflow of grace that was exhibited on the outside because that was what he was full of. Full of grace, splendor and majesty!

Therefore, what are you full of? What is seeping or shining through inside of you that manifests who you are? Are you masquerading or are you living a metamorphosis experience that not only transforms you but positively impacts the environment around you? Hopefully the latter.

Through the transformation process, you can now answer and identify how none of those initial questions that were stated in the introduction matter. Worrying about what the world thinks is beautiful vs. what is not, should no longer be a concern. Neither should the emphasis on what you should wear, how you should wear it and the make-up of your skin, hair or the like. I can no longer be concerned with what people think I look like or who I resemble. I and hopefully you as well, have learned that being transformed means living by the power within- your inner beauty and character. Let that be the main focus as you strive to have your metamorphosis take place. Only then can you see yourself, "beholding as in a mirror, the glory of the Lord, being transformed into the same image from glory to glory, just as the spirit of the Lord." Having a so called "pretty" face with a jacked-up attitude is not more acceptable. What IS acceptable is acknowledging that your confidence comes from something much greater than you, which researchers have found is the best predictor for anyone in order to be emotionally healthy and a stronger person. Acknowledging that you truly know "who you are and whose you are" is the best predictor of success and the confidence you need to be yourself.

Hill Harper also acknowledges it within his book the "The Wealth Cure". He understands that some people have the ability to command a room because of their "warrior light". He states:

In my speeches, I often talk about approaching life with a "warrior light." By this I mean the ability to exude a powerful and positive energy in all arenas. We are all familiar with the experience of seeing a person who "light's up the room", or who is a "star." I'm not talking about a celebrity. I'm talking about someone who seems to radiate from the inside. You've probably known one or two people like this. It's all about the energy they give off. When someone is a "star", they emulate light and energy and they do this wherever they go.

My husband always says that it is not always the outward appearance that is so appealing, but the confidence and knowledge of whom you are inside that makes someone beautiful. According to my husband, it is not necessarily the pressure from men to look a certain way. It is us females that feel in order for us to compete, we have to look, act or dress a certain way when the truth of the matter is, most men want us to look, act and dress like ourselves. Many black men dislike the added hair (weaves, wigs) and the like that make us seem artificial. My husband, for example, grew up with a lot of women around him and was exposed to the culture and experiences that came with being in a black salon. He stated that natural hair was always beautiful to him when he constantly saw all these women become something totally different after the beautician would finish their hair. It was such a turn off to him and he believed that the women were more beautiful when they embraced their own hair. He knew that whomever he was going to be with would have natural hair because he enjoyed when black women would embrace their natural beauty and texture of their hair and be able to exude that confidence. It was his preference. Other men say they are unable to embrace weaves and extensions also "because he never knew what he was going to get when he came home, and all of those things came off." I appreciate his honesty and the understanding that many other men feel the same way or differently. However, he also has unfortunately come across young men who'd rather date outside of their black race due to their inability of finding their race attractive or favorable. Or indicating that one particular type of women is the "quintessential beauty" since as Byrd and Tharps explain, "bombardment by images of Black females with long hair, coupled with historical condemnation of short natural hair, plays a great role in the mating rituals" (2011). In spite of the culture that sends the message to black women that (Byrd and Tharps, 2011) "we genetically lack a fundamental element of desirability" not all men are shallow in understanding where one's beauty lies, but are able to decipher that authenticity in any culture is attractive; inside and out. In addition, treating others in a respectful and genuine matter also completes the package. In the end, I believe it is all about your humble confidence and the value and self-respect that you exude within yourself.

I believe Hill Harper agrees with this understanding of knowing who you are and how to treat people the same wherever you are. He goes on to talk about those who "conform". He says:

Some people don't believe they are capable of producing this sort of energy. They feel they need props, a knot of cash in their pocket, or something they buy to adorn themselves with. This is where the term "bling" or "shine" came from. People feel that if they could dangle the most brightly shining jewels from their ears or necks, then the glow from the jewelry would convince others of their exaggerated worth. A guy might think that driving a flashy car will give him that kind of aura or, like my friend Andre, that making it rain in a club, possibly the most ignorant use of money ever, will elevate him in other's eyes....What these people don't realize is they have been seduced by the energy of money.

It's like the rich young ruler who asked Jesus what he needed to do to enter the kingdom of heaven. Jesus replies that he needs to commit to following the Ten Commandments. The rich young ruler then responds by acknowledging all of the good deeds he does in addition to keeping the Ten Commandments. Jesus then gives him a more difficult task that I'm sure Jesus knew was closer to his heart and challenged him with the task of "sell all your belongings and give it to the poor, then come and follow me". In that instance, the rich young ruler walked away with a solemn look because his worldly treasures were more valuable to him than letting go of his desires to follow Christ. Wow! How many of us see ourselves as this rich young ruler; Putting things, possessions, people and our agendas before Christ? Although the Bible gives us clear directions to "Lay not up for yourselves treasures upon earth, where moth and rust doth corrupt, and where thieves break through and steal; But lay up for yourselves treasures in heaven, where neither moth nor rust doth corrupt, and where thieves do not break through nor steal: For where your treasure is there will your heart be also" Matthew 6:19-21, it can be extremely hard living in a world that makes EVERYTHING so appealing.

It disturbs me immensely that this mentality can start so young when parents influence the minds of their children into thinking that their worth comes from what type of shoes they wear, what logo is on their jacket, or how many digital gadgets they have attained. It also hurts me to see how young it starts and how their understanding of self is being directly violated at such a young age!

Therefore, how do we avoid being sucked into the energy of money that Hill Harper previously explained? I believe it is when we realize, as he explains later in his book "that the bling that anyone purchases-jewelry, cars, and the audacious displays of cash, are ephemeral sources of shine that vanish the moment the person steps out of the Porsche or takes off the diamonds." He goes on to say that these things all "reveal something about us; they reflect our priorities. Most of us (unfortunately) are not entirely aware or comfortable with the entirety of the messages we are sending" (Harper, 2014). Maybe we should focus on "laying up for ourselves treasures in heaven" instead, as was suggested to us by Christ.

Therefore ladies, be adamant and up front, as to what you will accept as a respectable and honorable acknowledgement of yourself as a worthwhile person created in the image of God.

Guest Reflection

When I was going to a predominantly white school, all of the children would crack on me because I had 4 fingers on one hand, so I hung out with the children who were considered weird. I thought pretty meant to have long straight flowing hair. My mom put my hair in braids, but the other little girls had pig tails and pony tails so I always felt different. They always wanted to touch my hair and it made me feel very uncomfortable. Long and straight hair I guess is what I considered was beautiful at first. When I went to a predominantly black school in middle school, the teasing was worse. I didn't feel as bad about my hair because their hair was just like mine. Later I realized that beauty was how you carried yourself. I didn't necessarily get that from my mother. I watched this woman who always carried herself very well no matter how she was feeling. When I started going to her church I realized where she got her confidence from. She got it from her relationship with Christ.

-   Age 25

CHAPTER 4

WHERE DOES THIS CHANGE COME FROM AND HOW CAN I CHANGE?

Identify the root. A root, I believe, can begin at all stages of your life. You can develop a root early in your adolescent age. I believe you can even develop roots later in life as well, depending on the circumstances. It can also already be rooted in you from birth because of the generations before you. We all know that a root, in the sense of a plant is the initial anchorage that functions in absorption or storage. It is the underground part of the seed. The Merriam -Webster dictionary also gives the synonyms source, origin, ancestry. Therefore, any circumstance that serves as the start of an idea that formed in your understanding of self is identified as your root. As I stated in Chapter 1, I believe my understanding of my beauty and sense of acceptance of self wasn't challenged until that 4th grade experience. I'm sure the constant bombardment of what was considered beautiful by society's norms was infiltrated into my psyche by the TV shows, magazines, movies, toys and books that were surrounding me. However, although ever present as these surrounding sources were in my life, it wasn't until this direct 4th grade encounter and others like it challenged how I looked at myself and started the beginning of me comparing myself to others.

With that said how can we as a society and as individuals become aware of our place in helping others to discover their inner beauty just as we found our own? I believe it starts when we begin to realize that our words can either tear down or build someone up. Also, how we genuinely respond to someone as another legitimate thinking and feeling person. Whoever started the phrase "sticks and stones may break my bones, but words never hurt me" didn't understand the power of speaking life or death in a situation or to someone else. If God spoke in the very beginning and things just manifested on earth as He spoke them, that alone reveals the power of what words can do. As the Contemporary Christian song by Hawk Nelson states, "Words can build me up, words can break me down, put a fire in my heart or put it out".

Being mindful of what we're saying and how we're saying it to someone should not be taken lightly yet unfortunately is, especially in this day and age. You are looked at as soft, not having tough skin or too sensitive as someone continues to poke at, diminish and degrade any part of you. Instead of building someone's self-esteem it is easier for us, as a society, to diminish, make fun and laugh at their faults, mistakes and failures that at times can be very healthy for us as individuals. Every once in a while, you may need to laugh at the silly things you may have done and experienced in your life for your own sanity. Everything does not have to be so serious. However, there are times where this type of behavior is unhealthy and can instead become very detrimental to a person, especially when it comes from our parents and father's specifically. I think that we should instead try to find more ways to become more loving and aware of what we're saying to others as we go through the metamorphosis process of becoming more like Christ instead of choosing to conform to the norms of this world which allow us to acknowledge each other as anything less than what God has told us that we are. Loving yourself enough to work on your inner man or character is where your true beauty begins; which in turn means understanding that God loves that other human being just the same. Your actions towards that individual either helps them grow or tears down their growth of finding their inner beauty. As the late Maya Angelou stated in one of her famous quotes,

Words are things. You must be careful, careful about calling people out of their names, using racial pejoratives and sexual pejoratives and all that ignorance. Don't do that. Someday we'll be able to measure the power of words. I think they are things. They get on the walls. They get in your wallpaper. They get in your rugs, in your upholstery, and your clothes, and finally in to you.

Can you imagine how different this world would be if people would be more mindful of the negative dictations and condemnation that they spoke over and to one another and instead chose to speak life with positivity? How different would our children be if they heard more encouraging and truthful affirmations that built them up instead of tearing them down on a daily basis so that they truly knew they were loved? How different would families be if wives were constantly building up their husbands and treating them respectfully like kings while the husbands were truly loving their wives as the beautiful creation and queens that they were designed to be? How much more love would be expressed if we could all look beyond our differences and be able to look at that other person as a real thinking, feeling human being no matter what race, age, gender or class they belonged to?

I believe that was the reason we were put on this earth. To learn how to love others as Christ first loved us. That's why the next commandment that is closest to his heart, besides loving God with all your heart, mind and soul is to "love your neighbor as yourself." Loving yourself doesn't help when you're being torn down by your parents, father, mother and siblings. It definitely doesn't help if you're constantly being torn down by your surrounding environment either, including your peers, the media, the images and authority figures that are constantly around you. We all play a part in the uplifting and building up of another whether we like it or not. Therefore, we must be mindful of the words that are coming out of our mouth.

Undoubtedly, however, I believe that the most influential figure in a person's life is their father. Our relationship with our father on earth is a reflection of how we see our Father in heaven which hinders a whole generation of people who had absentee fathers, fathers who worked so much and never gave them any attention, fathers who were home but were so unsatisfied with their lives that they were still unable to be the fathers they needed to be. They weren't mentally present. How then do these children receive love from God when their life experiences and formation of "self" was challenged directly from the breakdown of their relationship with their father from the beginning? I believe it is up to us first to recognize it as in our own situation or life experiences. Only when we finally deal with and help ourselves can we truly recognize it and help others when we see it in them. As Eileen Fisher states in her book Embraced by the Holy Spirit (2009), sometimes we don't realize how "a distorted image of God the Father could hinder one's walk in His kingdom. Your spirit might be born again, but your soul can still carry within it painful memories attached to emotions that can prevent you from experiencing the great depths of the love of God."

I say this because I was so excited to help others when I decided to work on my own relationship with Christ, but I realized I couldn't help others as effectively when I wasn't able to be still and help myself first. Constantly I would ask myself would I have been so easily moved by my 4th grade peers' comments if I truly knew who I was in Christ first, or if I knew that my father thought I was the most beautiful girl in his eyes? Would I have needed that reassurance from my admirer in my class to reassure me that I was something pleasing in his eyes? What does that do to your confidence and assurance of yourself as you grow into an adult and these ideas are not already affirmed in your life? These and other similar ones are the questions I can ask and continue to ask myself until I'm blue in the face. Not until I decided to get over the past of what could have, should have, or would have taken place did true healing and moving forward take place.

Although I remember feeling attacked by others, due to a weird period in my life, where I thought I was significantly darker than the rest of my family and feeling pretty inferior about it especially when friends or friends of the family would playfully joke about it, I don't believe it would have affected my identity so much if it was constantly reaffirmed at home that I was still beautiful. Then I could accept who I was. Even though, I had totally supportive parents that believed in me and supported me in every dance recital, show, competition, youth day and the like, I was still looking for more. That more came from my father who I needed to reaffirm me as a darker hued young girl. What was it that I was missing? None of these questions would be answered until I could confront my dad about them. Gladly I received the response. Although jokingly yet unexpected he responded as if he didn't want me to become "big -headed" because I heard that I was cute so much and he believed that other people were saying it enough that I would naturally receive it. I appreciated my dad's honesty and willingness and availability of being present whenever I needed him. That definitely helped give me the confidence and assurance that God was always there whenever I needed him. I even appreciate the long talks, sermons and dissertations that he would lovingly spill out whether wanted or not. They each positively shaped my kind, easy going and understanding mentality of others. However, I realize that my eagerness to let it pass over or let it go when it came to others did not allow me to "let go" so easily. I still needed to hear my parents constantly reaffirm me as a darker-hued child which would have meant more to me than anyone else's constant celebration of my beauty.

Do not get me wrong. I know my parents genuinely love me. I do not blame my parents. I know, in many cases, this idea of beauty is a root concern that goes far beyond my generation, my parents, and grandparents and down the line and yet unfortunately still plaques our society today. Why would we think otherwise when slavery was abolished in 1865 and it is only 2015! Slavery lasted a good 245 years! (According to our history books). Accordingly, if we do our calculations correctly, it has only been 150 years since slavery has been abolished (95 years less than how long slavery lasted) and yet the Civil Rights Act for blacks took place in 1964. That was only 51 years ago! The very people who perpetuated racist ideas and ways of behaving to ostracize blacks may very well be alive today. If not, their offspring are certainly going strong and I find it very unlikely that everyone who has grown in such a hateful environment towards the black race are able to embrace blacks or those considered as "other" so lovingly as many profess to do now. Those ideas and ideologies were taught and ingrained in so many white children's little heads, they had no choice but to believe and receive the garbage that was poured into them unless proven otherwise as they've grown into adults.

I don't believe this strong hatred towards the black race or any race for that matter is a characteristic of everyone. However, to arrive at the notion that we are now a "colorblind" society that all of a sudden no longer looks at any person as just a color is deceitful. Pretending NOT to see color at all doesn't erase the history that took place because of it. As Patricia J. Williams states in her book Seeing A Color-Blind Future: The Paradox of RACE (1997), "This is a dilemma- being colored, so to speak, in a world of normative whiteness, whiteness being defined as the absence of color. The drive to conform our surroundings to whatever we know as 'normal' is a powerful force-convention in many ways is more powerful than reason, and customs in some instances are more powerful than law". This idea of "customs" Williams speaks about can be directly seen in Ray Jasper's case as he reflects on a book that he read in regards to whiteness being the norm but how it isn't considered by those who aren't directly affected until you say it like the following example:

Imagine you're a young white guy facing capital murder charges where you can receive the death penalty... the victim in the case is a black man... when you go to trial and step into the courtroom... the judge is a black man... the two State prosecutors seeking the death penalty on you... are also black men... you couldn't afford an attorney, so the

Judge appointed you two defense lawyers who are also black men... you look in the jury box... there's 8 more black people and 4 Hispanics... the only white person in the courtroom is you... How would you feel facing the death penalty? Do you believe you'll receive justice?

As outside of the box as that scene is, those were the exact circumstances of my trial. I was the only black person in the courtroom.

Again, I'm not playing the race card, but empathy is putting the shoe on the other foot.

As unlikely as this is for someone who is of Anglo Saxon descent, you can most likely have come up with a reasonable conclusion that the white person would seem highly outnumbered due to the lack of representation that he has with people looking like him. This isn't the predominant custom in the case of America however. Although, however diverse it is becoming in different authoritative arenas, there is still some sense of normality that reigns and is rooted in this overall scheme of life. It is known that out of the 1% wealthy Americans who occupy leadership and authoritative positions, the majority of them are still of an Anglo-Saxon descent. This is disturbing when the remaining majority are of another culture than the top 1% who are in authoritative positions. How likely is it that fair and accommodating rules are going to be made for this population?

How likely is the predominant custom that we are used

to seeing that indicates that "pretty" looks a particular way going to change? Not by being silent about the constant images that model it one way. Instead of embracing it as our own idea as a race, why can't we continue to redirect that idea of beauty like the few exceptions who went against the ideal "beauty" phenomenon.

One being a black model named Roshumba who was a popular Black actress and model of the late eighties and nineties and a major exception to the long-haired ideal. She was considered a dark model who wore her hair in a short natural cut, defying all the tenets of a Eurocentric beauty ideal. In Byrd and Tharps book, Hair Story (2011), she recalls an incident in an early 1990s Essence article of how a photographer told her to show up with her own wigs. She states, "I showed up without them and told the photographer, 'Either shoot me with my own 'fro or we don't do it'." Roshumba definitely made a revolutionary statement. Despite many efforts to keep that "normative" idea of what beauty is that had several articles still listing her as an exception to the majority rule, she still made a major statement that she is going to be shot as who she is and they were going to like it or not.

As a family-friend stated to me, "We receive our ideas of what is beautiful from those who have the money and the power." However, when you begin to embrace who you are in totality and others notice and embrace your difference as well, your unwillingness to back down begins to change the normal ways of thinking as we can see through People's Choice Magazine that has elected the beautiful Lupita Nyong'o as the most beautiful person in the world. Also through the new Dove ads and commercials that allow us to see all shapes and sizes of a women as beautiful, which I believe is refreshing since we come in different sizes.

So how do we holistically heal and deal with the pain that comes from 2 centuries of discrediting our worth as a race that has been told since the days of the first American newspapers and minstrels that perpetuated offensive racial images such as the pickanniny, coon and mammy that their hair is unacceptable and downright ugly? I doubt any progress will come if we continue to deal with it in silence. Yet, unfortunately for many years it has been silenced because "we all must pretend that nothing's wrong" or that we've come so far and what has happened in the past is over and done. Unfortunately, that is not the case for many. Byrd and Tharps reflect,

Black men's and women's psyches still value unkinky hair much more than the type that grows out of most black heads. Popular culture continues to be filled with Black women with long, or at least soft, moving hair. (Whether it be their own or a weave). Music videos overflow with light-skinned, long-haired women or continuing a trend that started in the early nineties, feature women who are of mixed heritage, Asian or Latina. Beauty advertising historically preys on the insecurities of those in its intended market, and the Black hair game is no exception.

Even though, Byrd and Tharps continue, "the late sixties and seventies 'Black is beautiful' movement was intended to liberate Blacks from enslavement to the concepts of 'good' and 'bad' hair. As the eighties progressed, it appeared that instead of being the beginning of change, those decades had been the exception to the aesthetic status quo." Yet we try not to talk about it or come up with some sort of resolve that will enable us to really heal. Williams states, "it is less and less fashionable these days to consider too explicitly the kinds of costs that slavery and colonialism exacted, even as those historical disruptions have continued to scar contemporary social arrangements with the transcendent urgency of their hand-me-down grief." For those reasons, we find it harder to embrace the beauty within and loving our natural hair. However, Williams offers a solution. "the ability to remain true to one self, it seems to me, must begin with the ethical project of considering how we can align a sense of ourselves with a sense of the world…Creating community, in other words, involves this most difficult work of negotiating real divisions, of considering boundaries before we can ever agree on the terms of our sameness" (1997).

To me that indicates that the mentality that states "I don't think about color, therefore your problems don't exist", contributes to the issue of not identifying there is a problem of declaring what an ideal beauty must look like. Until the problem is identified and realistically and thoroughly addressed, a true resolve for all parties who were affected won't take place. "We must be careful," as

Williams states, "not to allow our intentions to verge into outright projection by substituting a fantasy of global seamlessness that is blinding rather than just color-blind" (1997).

The fact that my parents' origin is from Virginia and my grandparents from North Carolina where racism and prejudice stands tall and bold even today should not be an experience I or my parents should brush under the rug. All of those experiences and privileges or non-privileges go into the making of who they are, the decisions they have made and were available to them to make compared to their counterparts who simply "privilege themselves as Un-raced". Several parents and older generation Blacks still maintain that un-straight hair will infringe on their children's and grandchildren's chances for economic and social survival because of the issues that race has brought. Today, that should NO LONGER be an issue. My grandmother even makes it evident when she can become overly concerned at the age of 92 about the texture of her hair as unfavorable and unmanageable. I understand now that the roots are deep and that my self-worth is not going to be and cannot be defined by others but I'm going to have to learn to be comfortable with myself because I have learned "who and whose I am". My dad constantly reminded me of this as I left toward whatever destination I was off to. Maybe that's why he held back in saying the things that I was longing to hear. He knew that was the main thing I should have confidence in and that was that I am a child of God and I belong to Christ and that He made me fearfully and wonderfully. That is where my confidence comes from now. Nothing else. He was wise enough to know that knowing who I am in Christ is far better and of much greater price than what I looked like on the outside.

As it states in Proverbs 31 about the virtuous woman we should all strive to become, "Charm is deceitful, and beauty is passing. But a woman who fears the Lord, she shall be praised." Whatsoever goes on with my outer appearance will eventually fade, but the way I treat someone, now that's what really has a lasting impression. That's what God really sees. He sees my beauty within and therefore that should be my focus and what I should put more emphasis in developing.

Guest Reflection

I believe I formed my view of what was beautiful when I was six and started going to school. I believed all of the girls with the long braids and light complexion were beautiful. The typical stereotype. I don't know where I got that from. It could have been the dolls. My grandmother gave me my first doll and it was a brown doll and I liked it. But when I was 12 I bought a white doll. A walky-talky, life-sized white doll because I always wanted a walky-talky life sized doll. I bought it myself, but I only played with it once. I don't know where I got the idea that light complexion and long hair was better. I barely watched TV growing up.

Everyone used to tell me I was beautiful growing up. They would come up to me and say, oh, what a pretty little girl you are. I wouldn't believe them. I always would look around and say, "Who are they talking to?" I think I didn't believe it until middle school when I started getting attention from guys.

My sisters would always make fun of me and say "You're so black! "You're black" because I was the darkest one out of them both. It was of course done in a negative way because being called black wasn't necessarily a good thing. That was when I was 7,8,9 and 10. We would get in fights and that's what they would say.

When I went to school I always had a problem with the length of my hair. I wanted to have long hair like my friends. I would pick friends who had long hair. I didn't stay with them just because they had long hair though. Later I realized that I had to choose friends based on the content of their character, like Martin Luther King said. If they weren't nice friends we soon parted our ways.

My dad said nothing. He went to work. He was so busy supporting the family and telling us how to act. He had nothing to say about my appearance or anything. It didn't bother me because he was working hard for us. We got no affirmation about our appearance except "Girl, why do you always have to tear your clothes up? You're a tomboy," because I always used to rip my clothes up climbing over fences after coming home from school. He would say "Can't you keep any of your clothes?"

I have no problem with my natural hair because I keep a perm. I had a fro in the earlier days but I only did it because everyone else was doing it. It was a social statement at the time. I think weaves, wigs and extensions are great for those who want to do it, but I don't like weave for myself or extensions. I think that's the beauty of black hair. We can do so much with it.

My dad gave me the confidence that I have by the example he set. He didn't have a lot of words but it was by his demeanor.

My advice to young girls is that it is not what you look like on the outside that matters but it is what you have inside and that comes from knowing who you are in God, who made you. He has a plan for your life and that's what matters.

-Age 64

CHAPTER 5
UNRAVEL YOURSELF

Understanding and acknowledging that nothing in your life happens by chance helps me to realize that maybe God allowed me to go through the things I did in my life so that I would have the opportunity to write about it like this experience and others to encourage others about the challenges we go through, knowingly or unknowingly. I undoubtedly don't believe that it was by chance that I struggled with my identity as a darker hued young girl in the way that I did to keep my experiences to myself. Whether it was to share it in this book, encourage other young women or ladies who I see struggling with the same issue, or just helping me to become humbler in myself and knowing how to kindly treat others despite first impression of outer appearance, it all goes into the making of who I am and whom God is creating me to be. Whether or not we want to accept the fact that our environment and surrounding facets that we grew up around deeply influences that makeup of who we are; we are all inevitably responsible in deciding how many of those deep-rooted ideas are our truths and should be embraced compared to what is actually horrifically false and must be exorcised.

I understand now that God wanted and still wants me to be sure of who I am. No matter how poorly treated I may be or feel because of outside factors, they are there to help me understand how it made me feel to be treated that way so that I will not make judgments or have biases towards others the way that others did me. I believe He did this because I constantly see a pattern where He kept me in a scenario where I always was challenged with having a great friend whom I was very close to and who always fit "the light skinned long hair" appearance. Each friend was very unique and extremely gifted in an area that we may have shared some common ground. However, we also had our gifts in areas that were unique to us as individuals. Although it was very tempting at times to give into jealousy or enviousness, the lesson I believed that I was to learn was to be confident in whom I was individually. As me, Stephanie. Although it proved to be very challenging because of how others would treat them because of their appearance, the process of not being jealous or feeling less than because of it remained. Where do you reach for this confidence when you at first felt that home unconsciously feels the same? It's hard to shake these jealous or envious feelings when you feel like there was no ground work for these feelings to be dealt with when everyone around you perceives to feel the same way whether they decide to admit it or not.

The only thing you can do is do your best at being who you are and were created to be. Never compromise your self-worth by behaving unfavorably just to attract the attention that someone else may get more easily. Taking out these feelings towards the one who is being treated favorably in your eyes isn't the answer either. God showed me to not harbor any hard feelings against those persons because it's not right. I realized after having a lot of resentment towards Shelby and choosing to have other friends didn't make it better especially when we were still friends. Shelby still was a nice, sincere, and great friend to have. Harboring any animosity or jealousy towards her doesn't make it better. Maybe Shelby was just a "star" and was more aware of her "warrior light" that was able to light up the room. More confidence is what I needed in realizing who I was and loving myself in every way in spite of how I felt treated. Hating someone else is just going to prolong the feelings that you have towards that person or others who resemble them and continue to lead into more jealous or envious feelings. It's better to admit these feelings to yourself first and if you feel the need, talk to someone who can help. Not someone who will just agree with what you are feeling. Don't let yourself get to where you in turn start hating the other person and conjuring up hurtful and mean things about this other person. Confide in someone who can understand where you are coming from or can just listen to help you let go of the hurt.

Anyone can feel this way at times no matter what walk of life they come from. It's not unique to you and you don't have to be so bold and confident about yourself when you honestly can feel tossed aside by others for whatever reason. Gabrielle Union even had to admit that she experienced being a mean girl before her very dear friend and life coach approached her about her unflattering behavior. I believe a lot of "hateration" is caused because people are just not real about their true feelings about a situation and they don't want to admit that someone had that much power over them to make them feel less about themselves. Gabrielle didn't feel better about herself or accumulate more wealth, security or a new man by blatantly and disrespectfully downing someone else. It wasn't until she admitted what was wrong with her that she was able to deal with herself to be better and receive what was really for her. True healing does not emerge when we hide our feelings about how someone makes us feel or how we really feel about ourselves. Honesty is always the best policy and admitting the truth behind your madness helps to release whatever was hidden in your heart in the first place. If you would not like it done to you, please don't try to justify doing it to someone else.

Embrace your change. Therefore, whether you struggled with your weight, your hair, your nose, your eyes, your ears or the like, the answer to finding the beauty within begins with truly accepting who YOU are. Do not accept what OTHERS think or say about you but listen to that inner voice within that tells you "Man looks at the outside but God looks at the heart." Really knowing who you are and developing a true acceptance of yourself is true freedom. Knowing that there is no other like you and being truly happy because that's whom God created you to be takes true growth and humility. It is freeing also not feeling like you have to compare yourself to any other person because you are now content with where you are today and loving yourself enough not to stay in a place where you focus on the negative responses of others but rather concentrate on what really matters... "The hidden man of the heart" YOUR BEAUTY WITHIN.

A morning devotional that inspired me to go against the idea of comparison said this:

...we will not compare ourselves with each other as if one of us were better and another worse. We have far more interesting things to do with our lives. Each of us is an original (Gal 5:25-26 TM).

By making comparisons, you're implying that God made a mistake in making you as you are. Furthermore, you're allowing others to define your worth, and giving them control over your self-esteem. That's too much power to give anybody! "Since we find ourselves fashioned...excellently...and marvelously...let's just go ahead and be what we were made to be" (Rom 12:5-6). Build on your God-given talents and stop coveting what others have. God made you what He wanted you to be, redeemed you and called you to fulfill His plan for your life. Until you stop comparing yourself to others, you'll never be able to give birth to the gifts He's placed within you. So, thank Him for making you who you are, and believe that He's transforming you day by day into the person He wants you to become.

With that said, BE TRUE TO YOURSELF! Live Freely, being you and do that UNAPOLOGETICALLY!

Let God Mold You! I like to compare this process of reaching one's inner beauty to an onion. I believe Joyce Meyers and others like her have come to the conclusion that God works on us continuously like an onion or dough being shaped into a specific figure. An onion grows in layers. Your growth, as far as your character goes, also grows in layers. We will never reach a place of perfection, but our growth should be continuous. A friend once told me, if you continuously find yourself in the same situation or find yourself in a difficult situation period, ask God what is the lesson He wants you to learn from this? I like to think of it as our preparation of how we should behave when we get to heaven.

We know that in order to get to the core of the onion we have to peel off layers and layers of the outer skin before we can get to the core. However, we spend most of our lives developing this thick skin to save us from being so emotional or easily moved when people attack us either verbally or physically. We're taught to develop some level of outer shell to keep us from being hurt. Meanwhile, all we're doing is covering up on the outside what God still can see that hurt us from within. It may not have fazed us in our understandings of self. However, there were some situations, comments and dealings that truly did affect us and was able to penetrate that thick skin that we developed over time that hit us right at the core.

I believe throughout our life God is constantly trying to get us, as we continue to grow, to remove that thick skin little by little, layer by layer, year after year, as he tries to get us to see the core of our situation to help us finally deal with what affected us in the first place. Just keep in mind that God would not have us waste our whole life dwelling on circumstances and experiences that would create a negative energy in us such as resentment, anger, jealousy and the like, but to dwell on yourself as being His creation; Move on to heal holistically, mind, body and soul to the point where you can love and forgive again. Also remember love and forgiveness is supposed to be unconditional not selective, and done on a daily basis. This conscious act performed daily creates a right spirit within us that not only improves our character but glorifies God. To God that is a great price. Something we can all strive to have as the late Ruby Davis leaves us with these WISE words "The kind of beauty that I want the most is the hard-to-get-kind that comes from within-strength, courage, dignity."

If you struggle with receiving affirmation about your beauty, within or without, I invite you to pray this prayer that my husband found and prayed for me. It comes from A Book of Prayers for Couples (2011) by Stormie Omartian. There is a female version that he prays for me as well as a male version that I pray for him. It is not unlikely that males can struggle with their self-image as well, due to the constant infatuation that our society focuses on in regards to the upkeep and building of one's body. Therefore, I encourage both males and females to discover their beauty within; their true identity in Christ.

Prayer for Her

Lord, where anyone in the past has convinced (wife's name) that she is unattractive and less than who You made her to be, I pray that You would replace those lies with Your truth. I pray that she will not base her worth on appearance, but on Your Word. Convince her of how valuable she is to You, so that I will be better able to convince her of how valuable she is to me. Show my wife how to take good care of herself. Give her wisdom about the way she dresses and adorns herself so that it always enhances her beauty to the fullest and glorifies You.

The King will greatly desire your beauty; because He is your Lord, worship Him.

-Psalm 45:11

Prayer for Him

Lord, I pray that (husband's name) will find his identity in You. Help him to understand his worth through Your eyes and by Your standards. May he recognize the unique qualities You've placed in him and be able to appreciate them. Enable him to see himself the way You see him, understanding that "You have made him a little lower than the angels, and You have crowned him with glory and honor. You have made him to have dominion over the works of Your hands; You have put all things under his feet" (Psalm 8:4-6). Quiet the voices that tell him otherwise and give him ears to hear Your voice telling him that it will not be his perfection that gets him through life successfully - it will be Yours.

We all, with unveiled face, beholding as in a mirror the glory of the Lord, are being transformed into the same image from glory to glory, just as by the Spirit of the Lord.

-2 Corinthians 3:18

I pray that you are blessed as you continue to work through your journey of unveiling your beauty within. I Do Believe I LOVE My Natural Hair!

Be Blessed,

Love Steph

DISCUSSION QUESTIONS

1. When do you think you formed your identity of what is beautiful vs. what is not? Who told you that you looked good and did you believe him/her?

2. Did you ever have a problem with your skin color? Why or why not?

3. Do you like girls with short hair or long hair? Explain which and why?

4. Who taught you what was beautiful? What was their insight about beauty?

5. What do you think of women who wear their natural hair? Is it considered ugly or beautiful? Why do you think this is the case?

6. What do you think about weave/wigs and extensions? Why do you think women wear it? Do you agree with the reasons?

7. What was the worst experience you had when someone attacked the way you looked. Did it hurt you or were you able to withstand their comments and know who you were?

8. Who/what gave you the confidence that you have?

9. Any words of wisdom to little girls or young men developing their identity?

10. When did you begin to truly love how you looked and the way you just are as a person?

Bibliography

INTRODUCTION

New King James Bible

CHAPTER 1

Byrd, A. and Tharps, L. (2001). Hair Story: Untangling the Roots of Black Hair in America. New York: St. Martin's Press.

CHAPTER 2

Channsin Berry, D and Duke, B. (2011) Dark Girls. United States: Duke Media.

Grover, J. (2013) Raising Resilient Kids. NJ Family. November 2013. http://www.njfamily.com/NJ-Family/November-2013/Raising-Resilient-Kids/ Nolan, Hamilton (2014) A Letter From Ray Jasper, Who is About to be Executed. Postcards from the Edge. http://gawker.com/a-letter-from-ray-jasper-who-is-about-to-be-executed-1536073598

CHAPTER 3

Harper, H. (2011) The Wealth Cure: Putting Money in It's

Place. New York, New York: Gotham Books-Penguin Group (USA) Inc.

Weirsbe, W. W. (1986). Real Worship: It Will Transform Your Life. USA: Thomas Nelson Inc.

CHAPTER 4

Fisher, E. (2005) Embraced by the Holy Spirit. Shippensburg, Pennsylvania: Destiny Image.

Patricia J. Williams, (1997) Seeing a Color-Blind Future: The Paradox of Race. New York: The Noonday Press.

CHAPTER 5

Gass, B and D. (2014) Stop Comparing Yourself With Others! The Word for you Today. 2014

http://www.thewordfortoday.com.au/devotional/stop-comparing-yourself-with-others

Omartian, S. (2011) A Book of Prayers for Couples. USA: Harvest House of Publishers.

STEPHANIE SHIDER

ABOUT THE AUTHOR

Stephanie Shider is the wife of Tylie Shider and mother of one beautiful girl named Mya. She received her B.A as a double major at Rutgers University where she studied sociology and dance through the Mason Gross School of the Arts. She immediately went on to receive her Master's in Education at Long Island University in Brooklyn, NY through a program she applied to called NYC Teaching Fellows. There she taught in Brooklyn while simultaneously attending graduate school for two years. Upon completion of her Master's program she found a job teaching closer to home(NJ) where she taught 2-4th grade for 4 years and continued serving in the Plainfield Community as a permanent sub and Teacher's Assistant teaching math to special needs students for another 2 years. She also became a licensed ministered and ministry leader of liturgical dance where she helped found DEW Ministries. She went on to complete her certification in Marriage and Family Therapy from North Central University. She currently teaches at a charter school in Brooklyn, NY, where she resides with her family. It is at this charter school where she developed the Girls on a Mission Curriculum in which this book is a part of. This book is the 2nd volume of her King's Daughters Series and she is looking forward to what more there is to come.

If you enjoyed Stephanie's story and would like for her to speak at your event or venue, you can reach her at:

stephanieshider@ladyonamission.org

Don't forget to check out Stephanie's website and follow, comment and share on her blogs or page:

www.ladyonamission.org

Stay in touch with Stephanie on Social Media

@StephanieShider

Please Like, Share your stories! I will be sure to comment back! Love and Be Loved! Peace and Hair Grease! Be Blessed!

Made in the USA
Middletown, DE
03 June 2022

66585700R10066